Henry's Clock

Acknowledgements

Thanks are due to the editors of the following publications in which some of these poems have appeared: *Chester Poets, Dog, Fat City, Iron, London Magazine, The North, Oxford Magazine, Peggy's Blue Skylight, Poetry News, The Rialto, Scratch, Second Draft, Smiths Knoll, Uncompromising Postions, The Wide Skirt.*

14 Ways of Listening to The Archers, published as a pamphlet by Smith/Doorstop Books in 1994, is reproduced here in a shortened, revised form.

'Meeting the Family' was broadcast on the late night Mark Radcliffe Show, BBC Radio 1.

Henry's Clock was the overall winner in The Poetry Business Book & Pamphlet Competition 1998.

Henry's Clock

Cliff Yates

Smith/Doorstop Books

Published by
Smith/Doorstop Books
The Poetry Business
The Studio
Byram Arcade
Westgate
Huddersfield HD1 1ND

ISBN 1-902382-21-8

British Library Cataloguing-in-Publication Data. A catalogue
record for this book is available from the British Library.

Typeset at The Poetry Business
Printed by Peepal Tree, Leeds
Cover design by Blue Door, Heckmondwike

Smith/Doorstop are represented by Signature Books, 2 Little Peter
Street, Manchester M15 4PS, and distributed by Littlehampton
Book Services Ltd, 10-14 Eldon Way, Lineside Estate,
Littlehampton BN17 7HE

The Poetry Business gratefully acknowledges the help of Kirklees
Metropolitan Council and Yorkshire Arts.

CONTENTS

For Gillian

1. *Tonight in Kidderminster*

Tonight in Kidderminster

begins under street lights and their word is Speed.
Two of them, chewing gum with their mouths open,
thumbs in their pockets and feet tapping.

The tall one sees me first, sees the hat. This hat
goes with the hair, the desert boots and jeans,
the shabby raincoat and ripped gold lining.

It goes with the sky before rain and just after,
and with one unforgettable night on Kinver Edge,
eight of us in the back of a mini van.

This hat is my dad's and I wouldn't sell it for fifty pounds.
*
They chased me for it and lost, turned left
into another story. Fiction.
It begins up an entry, shaking hands

full of someone's prescription.
Eyes that are needles
sewing the hem on tomorrow's shroud...
*
Or gramophone needles. The first record
is Stravinsky's *Soldier's Tale*.
The devil's guest, Private Faust,
has forgotten The Silent Princess.

He hums along to the drum solo
and dreams only of the fiddle
he traded for a book; words
he could not read, words he can't remember.
*

Next it's *4' 33' (for any instrument)*,
a bootleg of David Tudor
live in Woodstock, New York 1952.

The duff tape missed the rain
on the roof, traffic in the distance,
people angrily rising and leaving,

but detected the silence, four years
in the making. Listen; no
sound but the lid of the piano.

Tonight in Kidderminster our audience
is the night. The agitated stars cough less
and less discreetly, by the third movement

programmes flutter like moths. Barely visible
to the naked eye, the devil jigs
to the soldier's fiddle while The Silent Princess

wheels the plough across the night sky
and the pole star stays where it is.

1959

I have the 1950's in the palm of my hand.
It is a plastic Austin Seven,
inside my glove with the handbrake on.
Such a pale yellow, almost transparent.
There's smog on the way to school again.
My brother holds my hand across the road.

I like American comics; Jughead,
Mutt and Jeff, Sad Sack. What's a fire hydrant?
I re-read the punch lines. Sometimes
I get it, sometimes I don't. I even read
the adverts on the back, fill in my address.
There's a dead hedgehog in the road.
Paul turns it over with his foot – I dared him.
What's the 'zip code' for Birmingham?

Waiting for Caroline

Outside Readings on Blackwell Street,
bikes in one window, jokes in this one;
nail through your finger, Frankenstein,
invisible ink. She looked great
behind the gym at dinner time.
Her friends were in the long jump pit
out of sight of the dinner ladies,
holding down Andy and giving him love
bites. Outside Fletcher's, Mr Fletcher
humps potatoes, sings in Italian. She's late.

I've been set up. Like Cary Grant
in *North by North West.*
                              I'll hear it
before I see it; the crop duster –
out of the sun above the multi-storey,
dipping dangerously over the Seven Stars.
I'll make it to the Red Cross on Silver Street,
under the ambulance, hands over my ears ...
On the way home the fat man in the black suit
will climb on the Stourport bus with his cello.

I imagine her coming round the corner
by the Riverboat; she's run from the bus stop
but she's not sweating, she's smiling
like the girl in the Flake advert.

I'll tell John I didn't turn up
and if Frog says anything I'll hit him.

The Invisible Man

1.
On the back row in sunglasses and bandages,
sweating so much you can almost hear it,
I write on my desk in biro: TOTAL ECLIPSE,
NOWHERE MAN, HEAVY BREATHING.

Hottest day of the year – I take off my clothes,
unravel the bandages to the clicking of fingers
and stamping of boots as the school chaplain
searches for the bibles I've hidden.

He returns to my empty desk, sunlight,
dust motes and the silence you'd expect.

2.
Clothes at my feet, I shiver
in the air conditioning
as the personnel manager
examines my one qualification:
absence, void, the source
of a voice, the space before him.

The printers complain
the place is haunted; there are sightings
of my clipboard and stop watch
hovering near the Heidelbergs,
the hand dryer in the toilet hums
and stops for no reason.

I do a deal with the printers' union,
until management catch on.
What happened?
Maybe they 'saw' me,

in socks and a wrist watch,
chatting to the girls in Binding.

Perhaps it was the Dinner Dance
when I wore nothing
but lipstick. Or maybe
it was just the graffiti:
BEWARE THE SILENT MAN AND THE DOG THAT
DOES NOT BARK.

Ferret

My ferret is a very British ferret,
shy and retiring unless provoked.
I keep him in a special case, separate
from the snakes, strapped to the petrol tank
of my BSA 500. This gives me
a special feeling, not unlike wellingtons
with a dinner jacket, or pumps.

I tried to feed him sardines but he wouldn't.
I think he's got a hormone imbalance.
He chewed through the lawnmower
cable once. If it had been switched on
it would have served him right.
Then he found the bonemeal in the shed.
I heard him cough from the greenhouse and my wife
nearly fell off the ladder. The river's flooded.
It hasn't stopped raining since Christmas.

Visitors

Late one night in the middle of summer
Hart Crane knocks at my door. Water
streams from his hair.

He sits in the kitchen, warming his hands
on a coffee as about his feet a puddle gathers.
Shivering Hart Crane stares

at the floor tiles
as if playing chess, determined
to win before his argosy drowns.

Outside the window, the moth stirs,
raises its wings, settles again. Hart Crane
wipes his mouth with the back of his hand

and the doorbell goes. Captain Ahab,
wiping his boots on the mat. Water
pours from his beard.

Opposite Hart Crane, harpoon
between his knees, he flinches
at the white cup, will not look at the sugar.

Condensation gathers on the windows.
I dim the light, open the back door
to a solitary bat dive-bombing the lawn.

Herman Melville Was In The Garden

fastening twine to the bean canes,
hurling them like javelins over the fence

– next door's dog whimpered and whined.
Then he tied himself to the water butt

with the lawn mower cable. I had to cut
him free. Digging a trench, he fractured

the mains pipe, finished knee deep
in water. 'Okay,' I said, helping him out,

sitting him on the bench, 'tell me about it.'
He took a breath. 'Ishmael?' I said.

He began to roll up his trouser leg,
looking at me with that gaze of his.

Nathaniel Hawthorne softly groaned
but slept on in a deck-chair, under the apple tree.

Mohican

He's on the left with the mohican.
It used to be red but he got tired of the foreman
blowing kisses, clucking like a chicken
and whistling Little Red Rooster. The foreman
still waves coyly and whoops like an Indian
but better an Indian than a chicken.
The boss says he's a nice enough lad
but some of the customers
won't have him in the house
because he scares the children.
Now he has two of his own
and a haircut like his dad.
He drives a white Ford Sierra
and says what a state the world is in etc.
*

He doesn't mind what
his daughters' boyfriends look like
but he took a real dislike to one lad

not because he had long hair
but because he had long hair
as if he'd invented it.
*

She says, 'Listen. I wouldn't stick my legs
out like that, especially in those shorts
if I were you, they're not your best feature.'

End of August, he dismantles the boiler
and hoovers up the ants' nest,
empties the hoover bag into the compost

and watches the survivors,
smothered in grey dust,
some with fluff on their backs,

scatter, re-group, move off
quickly in no particular direction.

Hank

(for Brendan Cleary)

Woke up this morning in Arizona,
a filling station on the highway,
under someone's pick-up, dismantling the gearbox
which is a joke
because I'm the kind of bloke
who starts looking
for the left-handed hammer.

My name is Hank, I smoke roll-ups,
call you 'Bud' and have a wife called Gloria
who hangs endless items of clothing
on the washing line out front
when she's not in the kitchen
singing along to Country and Western
on the radio.

Men just turn up and say, 'How's it going Hank?'
I hammer repeatedly on the silencer
pretending I can't hear,
hoping they will go away
and thinking, 'Who the hell is this?
What does he know
about me that I don't know?'

I inspected the washing, worked out
that we have 8 children
between two and sixteen. Also,
judging from the patches
on the jeans and shirts
and the state of repair of the house,
we're not rich. And, judging from the way
I'm going at this gear box with a monkey wrench,
not likely to be.

Apples

The children won't sleep; we give them apples.
There is hardly enough light for these strange signs,
unfamiliar road markings, the distinction between
mile and kilometre. Our headlights find a farmhouse ...

Men and women in the loft hide inside barrels
with last year's apples, praying the rats keep still.
The young officer in the room below
slowly raises a Luger to the ceiling
and fires at random, here, and here. Blood
drips on his outstretched finger. Warm.
His men's boots clatter on wooden steps.

From barrels, hands push through to light,
apples bounce and roll across the floor,
machine guns rattle and grow hot.
Some stay crouched among the harvest,
breathing the sweet smell of bruised fruit
and listening for the sound of one bullet ...

Our youngest is so tired she can hardly
keep awake, let alone eat. She chews slowly
as if she is not used to eating,
hasn't eaten for a long time, has forgotten.

Sweet Sixteen

She goes her own way, will not listen,
stays up late, is easily influenced,
has friends we don't approve of.
She thinks she knows it all
but she doesn't, not by a long chalk.
She needs us; she says she doesn't but she does.
Sometimes she's like a cuckoo; we look at her
and think who is this stranger who eats our food,
locks herself in the bathroom and slams the front door?
She reckons the soul chooses its parents
on its journey towards liberation but when
she chose us she must have had dust
in her eyes or was drunk. Maybe she's right.
I said it's day to day that's hardest;
most of my friends lead lives of quiet desperation,
there aren't any signposts and we didn't
buy the guide book. She says being sixteen
isn't all daisies either, though sometimes she feels
a million years old, she feels the earth
spin and the tide change and one day it will
be okay but we have to trust her now.

When

To wait for the right moment then to strike,
like Dwight Yorke nutmegging the goalie
with the outside of his left, or the bin man
heaving his umpteenth bin bag into the moving truck,
regulation gloves making his hands sweat
as the astronomer's hands sweat,
training his telescope at a galaxy
like a sprinkle of flour on the breadboard,
the first time he's seen it since yesterday –
its light coming late, showing its appearance
as it was before Dwight Yorke, before polythene
bin bags that blow about the M6 terrorising
windscreens and wiper blades had been invented,
when we had metal dustbins for God's sake and tin baths.

Song of the English Teacher

Dreamed I married a girl in my fourth year class.
Her father poured me a drink and called me son.
He's 5 years younger than I am.
Down by the ocean she was thinking hard

and I don't blame her. When I was her age
the Americans were in Vietnam,
Sergeant Pepper had just been recorded
and Woodstock was about to happen.

The thirty years between us:
a reluctance to get up in the morning
the weight of the bag on my shoulder,
and all of my friends, well, older.

Leswell Street

She said, 'I've only been married 3 months
and I've already committed adultery.'
I felt sorry for Pete who obviously didn't know.
All I could think of was her at Frank Freeman's
on the rebound – all the lads wanting to
but not daring, apart from Geoff who
dared but only for three and a half minutes.

The end of a long night out, roe and chips
settling well on a few pints before the long
walk home up Birmingham Road, the house
asleep, all the noise inside my head, voices, pictures.

Voices, pictures, the brow of the hill
in the rear-view mirror, my foot off the accelerator,
cruising downhill in neutral, missing
the signposts. At least the tyres are new –
to me, anyway, part-worn from Germany.
Off a wreck, probably.

Like the one by the roundabout;
flames and black smoke pouring out
the driver's seat, the man in the suit
carrying a briefcase, signalling the traffic
to take a different route because
at any moment the petrol tank

Poem on the Decline of the Carpet Industry

You've given up smoking
and wander about the house in your vest.
You are working on a novel called *Breakfast*.
You get up early like Ernest Hemingway
and try to write a thousand words a day
on the typewriter but don't take time off
to fish in the Gulf Stream.
The most athletic thing you do is shave
though some nights you go for a long walk with a pram
that you fill with firewood from the building site.
The free newspaper comes in useful for lighting the fire.

Your parties are legendary;
videos of Dixon of Dock Green
on a huge black and white television
to the sound of Captain Beefheart, Chicken Shack
and Duster Bennett live at Frank Freeman's.
Let's applaud the perfect moment;
George himself saluting the camera
under the famous black and white blue lamp
to the opening bars of 'Autumn's Child'.

Saturday Afternoon

Walking along Swansea Uplands
I recognise Saturday afternoon.
I'm surprised

and try to think what it is
that makes it
unmistakeably Saturday afternoon.

September. Leaves losing
their grip, even the cars
humming something different.

Now Bill is a fat man and noisy,
walks in a room and the windows
rattle. Appears when you least expect him.

'Bill! Come over here,
say hello to Saturday afternoon.'

Henry's Clock

Henry's alarm stops ringing when you shout.
He likes to set it for one minute
and shout 'STOP!' It is satisfying

but not intelligent. If you shout,
'CARRY ON!' it stops. It does not discriminate
between happiness, anger and despair.

If you like, you can shout,
'THE RIDERS ARE TRAMPLING THE NIGHT
ON THEIR TERRIBLE SHINING HORSES!'

Oakworth

December. It's been dark all afternoon.
Telescope over his shoulder, my brother
climbs gingerly the steps of his new garden.
We wait in the light from the kitchen,
watch the beam of his pencil torch.
The kids are so patient. It's unbelievably cold.
Turn off your torch, stand here, that's right
not too close, you don't need your glasses.
He shows us Jupiter with its bands of clouds
and Saturn with its rings and moons.
Jewels. They're so small and intense.
I want to watch them forever.
The motor hums as the Earth turns.

Our mother climbs the treacherous steps
to see for herself, holding onto my arm.
However does he manage? she says.
She's staying for Christmas. I leave her on the sofa
watching television in front of the gas fire.
Driving back over the Pennines it starts to snow.

The Bed's Not Made

It was routine like blacking your boots
or my dad wearing a tie under his overalls.
Now we leave the duvets all day,
maybe shake them before climbing in.
Pillows dented in the daylight.

'She's not going upstairs is she,
the bed's not made. Besides,
I'd like to see you cook *me* a meal
if *my* publisher came to lunch.
If he was male, good-looking ...'

She cooks pasta, garlic because I won't be
going back to work. *Stollen* from Aldi.
'Was it stolen?' The kids groan.
'Would you like to smoke?
I was going to arrange scaffolding
so you could climb on the roof and feel at home.'
It's that kind of conversation. We're all in the kitchen,
crowded round the cooker, windows streaming.
Gill serves quickly, has to be back at work
in three quarters of an hour.
She's right. I'd probably poison the bastard.

I'm Sorry, I Didn't Sleep Last Night

What time is it? Rule one: don't look at the clock.
Rule two: listen to your breathing. Boring.
Rule three: don't worry – just lying there
is two thirds as good. Who are they kidding?
You know it's bad when your feet get hot;
push them out from under the duvet
and they're straight away cold.

She's asleep. Whatever happens
she sleeps like a little girl,
always. She turns over. Her breath
hot in my face. How can you turn
over like that and still sleep?
So much movement and turning.
If I so much as stretch out
my legs, she sighs. I turn gently,
holding my breath. My heart
beats, nothing to do with me;
a live thing in a bucket on my left.

Next day I yawn and yawn.
Where do these yawns come from?
Luke's already at his desk, doing Maths.
'It's hard this, Dad. Look, there's a sequence
but I don't know what it is.'

There's a sequence, it comes
and goes. The yawns seize my gut
and I gape, my eyes fill with water
and reality is wide and empty. All I want
is curled sleep, tucked warm and slow,
but daylight hours stand upright.
I pass them one by one,
black figures in a dry land.

Dance

(i.m. Chris Dance, 1951-1998)

Thomas already at college, Gill at work,
Luke playing The Levellers on his stereo,
Ruth pouring coffee into my Villa mug
in a cereal bowl in case it spills,
her cardboard boxes and egg cartons
by the front door for Art and even when
I'm not thinking about it I'm remembering,
the memory colouring the day like a colour
wash. I hadn't seen her for thirty years but
still remember her walking away from us
up Gheluvelt Avenue in her prefect's blazer
with her sister, looking back and
grinning at one of my stupid jokes
at four o'clock on Friday in September,
the sun breaking through and already I'm
turning away because me and John
have our lives before us and there's
nothing like nor will there ever be
the thought of Friday night.

On The Difficulty of Learning Chinese

My father met my horse when he was 19.
She was 12, but you only had to see them together.
He was handsome and she was incomparably beautiful.

She also had the most wonderful singing voice.
Father said she could sing the stars out of the sky.
My friends would come round just to be with her.

She was like a second horse to them.
When I was eleven she gave me my horse scarf.
Such a wonderful texture; cool in summer, warm in winter.

She made it from an old shirt belonging to my father.
He would never throw anything away.
But he was so angry. It was the first and last time

that I ever heard him use the word linen.

Reel-to-Reel

1.
Bought for seven pounds from the old lady
who lived by the cricket ground.
We try it out in John's
front room, sing 'When I'm sixty four'
into the mic, or try to, but can't
get past the first two lines for
laughing at our ridiculous voices,
the sound of our laughter,
at his mother, listening in the hall.

2.
We listen to the whole of the tape to catch it –
my mother insists he's on here somewhere
and then we find him.
He's saying something,
in the next room, one Christmas.
What he's saying is not important,
not the point.
It's just the sound of his voice,
unmistakeable, exactly like it was.

2. 14 Ways of Listening to The Archers

Clara

'Sweet, Sir?' 'No thank you. I've just eaten
a little boy.' He stands at the classroom door,

rubbing together big hands. 'Poetry
tomorrow Clara. Poetry!' Clara

has other plans. She's seeing Andy who's
doing Sociology and English at the Tech. Saturday

he took her on the terraces, Villa Park.
She stood behind him, warming her hands

in the back pockets of his Wranglers.
Later they shared a hot dog at the fair,

started at either end, met in the middle.
On the bus home they sat upstairs at the back,

smoking French cigarettes. He cupped both hands
around her goldfish in its plastic bag.

She peeped through the cracks, wanting it to sleep
in the pink dark. Tomorrow it's his place;

his mum's out for the day. He'll read her
his essay on *The Crisis of Identity of the Post*

Industrial British Working Class. They'll lie
together in front of the electric fire,

listening to Van Morrison. Later, upstairs,
they'll run a warm bath, set the goldfish free.

Playing for Time

Arms out like sleepwalkers, the fourth year
stumble down the corridor, pretending
to be blind for English. In the toilets they skid
on wet tiles, make ghost noises, pretend to be drunk.

Next door it's trigonometry.
Mr Russell draws a ladder on the board,
talks about window cleaners, tangents,
flexes his cane and calls it George.

Here in RE the school chaplain
has just smacked Tony Bishop on the head
for making a high-pitched whining noise
while he was dictating notes on Jeremiah.

He's not having a good day.
We have hidden his cane
behind the map of Jerusalem.
Earlier, a grain of rice from my biro, aimed

at the 4 inch wooden cross balanced
on the bookcase, landed on his mark book
in a pool of spit. He made me empty my pockets.
I had enough rice to make a pudding.

Over the bike sheds the sun
shines through the fog like a Trebor mint.

Apprentice

We stopped the machines at twelve.
Now it's past one and I'm losing
count.

The managing director is telling
a dirty story in a collar and tie,
his smile

dripping into whisky and dry.
The fairy lights play
havoc

on his Brylcreem.
The dartboard will not keep still. My dart
bounces

off the light, sticks
in the rubber mat. Miles away on my
left,

a slow hand
clap. Outside, the cold is a
wet

dishcloth. I lean
over the fence, top of the embankment.
'Well done lad.'

The voice –
over my shoulder, a pint of beer
in its fist.

Bricks in the Snow

After the factory – 'A' levels at the Tech.
For six weeks I didn't know
where I was.
The Sociology lecturer told us
to call him Rob.

'That's why you're here,' he said,
grinning through his beard,
'so you won't have to do that.'
Outside, builders
humped bricks in the snow.

Outside, a bloke threw bricks
to his mate up on the scaffolding.
They flew red
through falling snow.
Every one caught clean.

When I return, Rob is fatter
than I remember – beer.

Borth

We're woken by tearing grass, cow breath
and the sun, orange through the walls of the tent.
We swim in summer rain – the sea is warm
as bath water. The farmer drives us home

shivering in his trailer like mermaids
in a carnival. We watch forked lightning
over the railway track, count the miles
in seconds, then take turns to dip fingers

in the nightlight and peel off fingerprints,
trying to get a perfect one. In the white cafe
on the edge of town I fry chips, boil peas,
while you serve meals for eight pounds a week

and all we can eat. My clothes are stiff with grease.
The owner's mother at the sink has no English
or Welsh. She nods and smiles, chatters in German,
gives us pennies to spend, like grandchildren.

We drink cold Double Diamond in straight glasses,
smoke before breakfast. At nights I lie awake,
listen to your breathing. You talk in your sleep
but I can't make out what you're saying.

Back home in Kidderminster the juke box
in the Green Man still plays the same tunes.

Telescope

November, 2 am, frost. My brother,
on a sun lounger in the back garden,
is dressed for it; balaclava, socks on his hands,
two overcoats and a blanket. He sips scalding coffee
from the flask and, when he hears me
ease the gate, carefully wipes his glasses.

Just back from a party that didn't get started,
I pull up a deckchair as he aims the telescope
like a mortar above Birmingham Road
at a patch of white somewhere in Andromeda.
Two hundred thousand million stars. It's like
powdered light or sherbert with light behind it.

I give him the last of my chocolate,
take off my shoes and socks and walk on the grass.

The Day the Lawnmower Caught Fire

My brother had shut himself in the garage
with the snooker table and six banana sandwiches
and was perfecting his opening shot
in the half-light from the one grimy window
in the far corner. You could hear the balls snap
even over the whine from the lawnmower.

I had just turned my back on the lawnmower
leaving it to cool by the rhubarb while I had
five minutes with *Roads to Freedom* on a deckchair.
The lawnmower, sick of being pushed around,
neglected and made to chew wet grass with blunt blades,
reached a decision and looked happier in flames
than it had ever looked. Even the wet grass
around it went black and smoked in sympathy.

from *The Pond Poems*

('... a three-headed bloke lives in the pond. He comes
out at midnight and sits there, singing...' from 'Socks',
by Ian McMillan)

Dear Son

You will have realised by now
that it's a lonely business
living in a pond, having three heads.

It's expensive on cigarettes,
three mouths, expensive on health –
two lungs. Avoid barbers' shops;

haircuts take longer, lead
to unnecessary questions.
For variety, keep one head

unshorn, another shaved,
the third under a hat.
Buy two hats at a time, preferably

with straps. Others tend to float
away when you submerge. You might
find, incidentally

that the novelty
of untangling fish-hooks
from your hair wears a bit thin

in the end. Always remember
our song, the one I sang
over and over, stoking your heads

when you were a bambino.
Above all, do not return
to your mother.

She is trying to lead
a normal life. Unlike us
she's not nocturnal. Has

no reason to be. One day
they might bring her to see you
but don't count on it.

Dear Husband

I've seen our Graham, visited his pond
last night. Just after dusk he surfaced,
danced, sang the song. He had it
exactly right, you'd have been proud.

It's uncanny, each of his three heads are just
like yours, twenty, thirty years ago.
I know what you will say, I know
I shouldn't have gone. I didn't think

they'd let me, not after Kevin!
His eyes were just the same; I remembered
him gazing at us as he fed, two mouths
at a time. My sore breasts! Remember?

Afterwards you would carry him room to room
cradling his heads in your strong arms
and, when you thought I couldn't hear,
you'd sing him the song.

You knew he would need it; you knew
it would be like this. I should have listened.
Now all I do is dream of you both
in your murky depths. I long for you

across the table at breakfast, hair dripping,
one head munching toast, another reading
out something amusing from the Guardian
letters page, the third dozing, murmuring

in fond watery dreams.
I know it's impossible but I wish
you'd come home. Together we'd dig a new pond,
a huge one, fill it with weed and fish.

Clare and Kevin

Picture it; the short-cut through the woods,
dusk; I hear splashes from the pond then singing.
I listen but can't make out the words.

I see him before he sees me, which is surprising
because he has three heads. He sits on the bank,
feet in the water, wet but not shivering

in dungarees and t-shirt. He moves his hands slowly
to the song. One head wears a woolly hat,
one's shaved, the other has a beard – it sees me.

The singing stops. I lean back against a tree,
touch bark with my fingers. He moves his feet
in the water. The moon in the pond breaks up

then forms again. 'I'm Kevin,' says the bald one.
'That's right, Kevin,' says the beard, winking.
It felt as if the pond was listening.

Kevin

The pond is clear and full and bright
and the ocean's a pond, my dad once said.
I'm tired and it's late, I'll be gone tonight.

We've slept all day and could sleep all night.
Dream on my love while I stroke your head.
The pond is clear and full and bright

Through a gap in the curtains the last of the light
plays in your hair and measures our bed.
I'm tired and it's late, I'll be gone tonight.

Our first night together was dynamite.
You cradled my heads in your lap and said,
'Our pond is clear and full and bright.'

We'll no longer live by candlelight;
tomorrow I'll sleep on the lonely sea bed.
I'm tired and it's late, I'll be gone tonight.

The Harley is ready, it's almost night,
I'll wake you with kisses, sleepyhead.
I'm tired and it's late, I'll be gone tonight.
The pond is clear and full and bright.

Get Me Flowers

And when you give me them,
don't keep asking are they all right.
Surprise me. Get something exotic
like lilies, if they're not too far gone.

Get them in your lunch break
and not from that grocer's
by the bus station. Go mad.
Make me feel good.
Remember the double camomile
from the Half Moon wholefood shop;
you can do it if you want to.

If it's daffodils don't choose
the big long trumpet sort
and say I could only find these.
Look carefully before you buy them.
Don't get back, notice they're a bit droopy
and say sorry I didn't realise,
like the roses you bought in Liverpool.

I want something natural, with a smell
but not freesia in polythene
with soggy cotton wool in the bottom.
Just because it's your favourite flower
doesn't mean it's mine.

Know what I'd like?
To be in that position
(I don't suppose you'll ever do this)
like in films when the man buys
everything in a flower shop
and she's got so many
she doesn't know where to put them.

Life and Soul of the Party

The life and soul of the party?

Come on
you've never been
the life and soul of the party
have you?

I mean
you can't honestly say you've ever been
the life and soul of the party
can you?

Let's be honest
I didn't marry you because you were
the life and soul of the party
did I?

Meeting the Family

He says something
witty
about the budgie.

They smile.
He is smiling so much
that his cheeks ache.

He crosses his legs
and kicks the budgie
into the fire.

She screams.
It is not
a good start

to the evening.
It is not easy
to make conversation

with charred feathers
floating
about the room.

Naked, the Philosopher

Pale, thin and naked, the philosopher
stands in the door of his flat, yawning.
His exams are in two weeks. It's twelve noon
and his teeth are still in the glass.

His mushrooms have left their gro-bag.
In his hot dark room they sprout
white between books.

Midnight, he leans against the door frame,
muttering. At two in the morning
he's playing chess and drinking vodka,
eyes watering in the smoke.

He's the one without the invitation
but on every picture. On this one,
bride and groom either side the oak,
he's top right, bending at the waist,
reading the words on the stone.

14 Ways of Listening to The Archers

1.
There are archers
and there are Archers.
Forget bows and arrows.
I am talking soap.

2.
In my white Reebok trainers
and famous shorts,
I practise my new walk
along Coventry Street
listening to the Archers
on my Sony Walkman.

3.
There are some things you always do
and some things you never do.
Listening to The Archers, we like to think,
falls into one of these categories.

4.
I eased the metal and the lock gave
so I turned the handle and pushed.
No alarm. I could hear the woman
next door. She was running a bath
and listening to The Archers.

I was nearly finished in the kitchen
when the telephone started ringing.
I stood at the window, watching an old blackbird
digging in the lawn for worms.
The telephone rang 13 times.

5.
What do they do
when we're not listening?

6.
Ronnie drives his white Ford Capri
at 40 mph on Black Rock Sands in the rain.
It had to happen, now it has –
the engine has stalled, the tide's coming in
and he's completely out of WD40.

He turns on the radio in desperation
as salt water licks his hub caps.
The last thing he hears as he runs for help
is the signature tune of The Archers
through the window he left open.

7.
Aliens orbiting Earth and taking notes
tune into The Archers, for instance.

8.
It's amazing the size of a boat
you can shift on greased planks
with wire ropes and snatch blocks.
Look at this one; it's 40 feet –
that's a few tons of boat.

The foreman fills a bucket of water
ready to pour on the planks
from the tap outside the workshop.
Inside, someone has left on the wireless.
Listen, it's The Archers.

They could have shifted the pyramids
like this, the foreman reckons.

9.
'Hello Ned, me old pal, me old beauty...'

Walter Gabriel, Ned Larkin, where are you now?

10.
I am doing my Maths homework
on the table in the living room.
It's Thursday. I have Maths
Tuesdays and Thursdays. There are fifteen
Maths homeworks left before Christmas.
Tonight it's Simultaneous Equations.

At 7.30 it's 'Top of the Pops'
and at 8.00 it's 'The Man from Uncle'.
I prefer Illya Kuryakin to Napoleon Solo,
John Lennon to Paul McCartney and Tonto
to the Lone Ranger. The Archers is on
in the kitchen where my mum is washing up
and my dad is blacking his boots.

I can hear it through the hatch – the most
depressing programme on the radio
is 'Sing Something Simple' on Sunday afternoons.

11.
Forget Coronation Street,
forget Eastenders, Brookside,
Emmerdale, Neighbours, Home and Away.
Who needs a telly anyway?

12.
Graham is being nice to his girlfriend
in the imitation leopard-skin nightshirt
given to him by Mike the American,
Justin is cooking an omelette
in the kitchen on his new frying pan
that he keeps in his wardrobe,
I am pretending to write an essay
on *The Function of the Chorus in Greek Tragedy*,
Paul is listening to The Archers
while cleaning the paintwork on the landing
and Steve is doing yoga in the pantry.

13.
That cow sounds realistic doesn't it?
I said, that cow sounds realistic, doesn't it?
How do you think they do that?
A recording, possibly?
Are you listening?

14.
Right after their bath, the beautiful couple
kneel in front of the French windows
overlooking the white garden.

He undoes her dressing gown, she arches her back.
Someone turns on a radio upstairs.
It has stopped raining at last.

Cliff Yates was born in 1952 and grew up in Birmingham and Kidderminster. He left school at 16 and did a variety of jobs before returning to full-time education. He has degrees from Swansea and Warwick Universities. He lives in Skelmersdale with his wife and three children, where he teaches at the Maharishi School.

His pupils are extraordinarily successful in achieving national awards for their writing. He is currently Poetry Society poet-in-residence for Secondary Education, and his resulting book, *Jumpstart: Poetry in the Secondary School,* is published by the Poetry Society.